THE BEST NFL
DEFENSIVE PLAYERS
OF ALL TIME

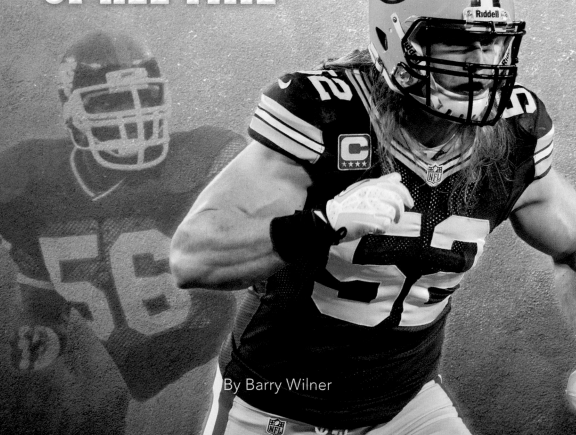

By Barry Wilner

Printed in the United States of America,
North Mankato, Minnesota
052013
092013

 THIS BOOK CONTAINS AT LEAST 10% RECYCLED MATERIALS.

Editor: Chrös McDougall
Series Designer: Christa Schneider

Photo Credits: Paul Spinelli/AP Images, cover (left), 1 (left), 23, 53; Dave Stluka, cover (right), 1 (right); NFL Photos/AP Images, 7, 11, 13, 15, 17, 19, 21, 31; PS/AP Images, 9; Doug Mills/AP Images, 25; Al Golub/AP Images, 27, 29, 41; Charles Krupa/AP Images, 33; Four Seam Images via AP Images, 35; Kevin Higley/AP Images, 37; Kevin Reece/AP Images, 39; Paul Jasienski/AP Images, 43; Greg Trott/AP Images, 45; Nick Wass/AP Images, 47; Perry Knotts/AP Images, 49; Rob Carr/AP Images, 51; Kevin Terrell/AP Images, 55; Tom Hauck/AP Images, 57; Jim Mahoney/AP Images, 59; Jim Prisching/AP Images, 61

Library of Congress Control Number: 2013931959

Cataloging-in-Publication Data
Wilner, Barry.
 The best NFL defensive players of all time / Barry Wilner.
  p. cm. -- (NFL's best ever)
Includes bibliographical references and index.
ISBN 978-1-61783-908-5 (lib. bdg.)
ISBN 978-1-62143-003-2 (pbk.)
1. National Football League--Juvenile literature. 2. Defense (Football)--Juvenile literature.   I. Title.
796.332--dc23

2013931959

TABLE OF CONTENTS

Introduction 4

Dick "Night Train" Lane 6

David "Deacon" Jones 10

Dick Butkus 14

"Mean" Joe Greene 18

Lawrence Taylor 22

Ronnie Lott 26

Reggie White 30

Bruce Smith 34

Rod Woodson 38

Deion Sanders 42

Ray Lewis 46

Ed Reed 50

Patrick Willis 54

Clay Matthews 58

Honorable Mentions 62

Glossary 63

For More Information 63

Index 64

About the Author 64

INTRODUCTION

It's often been said that offense sells tickets, but defense wins championships.

Through the years, the National Football League (NFL) has had hundreds of star players on defense. Some were great pass rushers or run stoppers. They would sack quarterbacks and stop running backs in the backfield. Others were linebackers who could do almost everything all over the field. And then there were the defensive backs—cornerbacks and safeties. They were speedy, smart guys with short memories. The last point is key, because at some point, they all were beaten for big plays. They had to bounce right back on the next snap.

Here are some of the best defenders in NFL history.

DICK "NIGHT TRAIN" LANE

The receiver running across the field to catch a pass knew what was going to come next. He was going to get hit by the Night Train. And it would feel like being run over by one.

Dick Lane was given his nickname by a teammate who thought Lane liked the song, "Night Train." What Lane really liked was running through receivers like a locomotive.

Lane, who played offense before reaching the NFL in 1952, is most remembered for his tackling style. He had two moves that are no longer allowed, in part because of him. He often brought down a ball carrier by the face mask. That was legal when he came into pro football. He also used the "clothesline" tackle, bringing his arm across his body from the side, into a receiver's neck or helmet.

Dick "Night Train" Lane was one of the NFL's hardest hitters during the 1950s and 1960s.

After spending four years in the Army, Lane asked the Los Angeles Rams for a tryout. They saw his speed, quick reactions, and power. So they signed him— but for the defense. That's because back in the 1950s, receivers usually were faster than defensive backs. And the Rams wanted to change that.

"When you lined up against him, you were in for a tough day," said Hall of Fame receiver Tommy McDonald. "God should never have given him that kind of speed."

Lane wound up with 68 interceptions and five touchdowns in his career. He also made seven Pro Bowls. Fans remember him most, however, for being the Night Train.

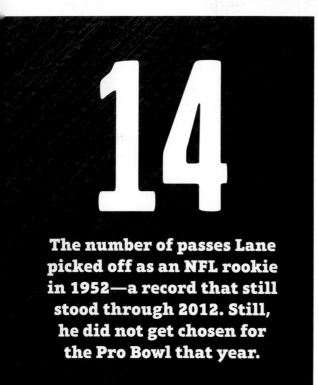

14

The number of passes Lane picked off as an NFL rookie in 1952—a record that still stood through 2012. Still, he did not get chosen for the Pro Bowl that year.

Dick "Night Train" Lane, playing for the Detroit Lions, leaps into the air to intercept a pass during a 1962 game.

DICK "NIGHT TRAIN" LANE

Position: Defensive Back

Hometown: Austin, Texas

College: Western Nebraska Community College-Scottsbluff

Height, Weight: 6-foot-1, 194 pounds

Birth Date: April 16, 1927

Teams: Los Angeles Rams (1952–53)
Chicago Cardinals (1954–59)
Detroit Lions (1960–65)

All-Pro: 1956, 1961, 1962

Pro Bowls: 1954, 1955, 1956, 1958, 1960, 1961, 1962

DAVID "DEACON" JONES

In college, David "Deacon" Jones was so fast he would outrun tailbacks. So when scouts for the Los Angeles Rams looked at college running backs and saw film of Jones catching them from behind, they were impressed.

Even more impressive was Jones's work as a pro. If sacks had been an official statistic when Jones played, he might have set a mark that no one would reach. And he would have deserved it. After all, Jones first termed the word "sack" for knocking down a quarterback.

Former Rams teammate and Hall of Famer Merlin Olsen said, "There has never been a better football player than Deacon Jones."

David "Deacon" Jones was a member of a Los Angeles Rams defensive line known as the "Fearsome Foursome."

Jones made a living in enemy backfields. He went from a fourteenth-round draft pick to being one of the most feared pass rushers in the NFL. In both 1967 and 1968, Jones was voted the league's top defender.

"I came as close to perfection as you can possibly get," Jones said.

Jones wasn't only a master of quarterback sacks. He recovered 15 fumbles in his career and forced two safeties. He also was a leader on the Rams' "Fearsome Foursome" defensive line.

Yet for all his great play, Jones never made it to a championship game. He was, however, a regular in the Pro Bowl. And when he was traded to San Diego in 1972, Jones did just as well for the Chargers, again making the Pro Bowl. He retired two seasons later, ending his career as one of the greatest defensive players the NFL would ever see.

5

The number of games Jones missed in his 13-year career. He played in 191 games overall, which is an almost impossible achievement for such a hard position.

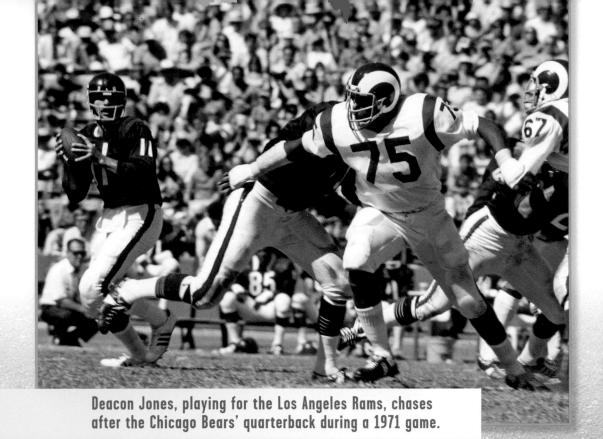

Deacon Jones, playing for the Los Angeles Rams, chases after the Chicago Bears' quarterback during a 1971 game.

DAVID "DEACON" JONES

Position: Defensive End

Hometown: Eatonville, Florida

College: South Carolina State University, Mississippi Valley State University

Height, Weight: 6-foot-5, 272 pounds

Birth Date: December 9, 1938

Teams: Los Angeles Rams (1961–71)
San Diego Chargers (1972–73)
Washington Redskins (1974)

All-Pro: 1965, 1966, 1967, 1968, 1969

Pro Bowls: 1964, 1965, 1966, 1967, 1968, 1969, 1970, 1972

13

DICK BUTKUS

Just the name Dick Butkus sounds like someone who should be making hard hits on the football field. And nobody hit harder than the Chicago Bears' linebacker. Some consider Butkus to be the greatest linebacker in NFL history. Others take it a step further. They say he was the best defensive player in NFL history.

Every opponent feared being tackled by Butkus. The Bears' defense was nicknamed "Monsters of the Midway." And Butkus was the man in the middle of it all.

The NFL didn't keep statistics for tackles when Butkus played. However, it's believed he led the Bears, and possibly the league, in tackles for nearly all of his nine seasons. But he wasn't just a tackler. Butkus also dropped back in pass coverage, making 22 interceptions.

Linebacker Dick Butkus is still a legend in Chicago after his nine seasons at the center of the Bears' defense.

Butkus had a career-best five picks in his rookie season. And he always seemed to find the ball. Butkus recovered 27 fumbles in his career, many of which he forced himself.

Butkus had surprising speed for such a rugged player. His coach, the legendary George Halas, said Butkus was as smart as anyone he ever coached. So from where did the third overall draft pick in 1965 get his edge?

"If someone on the other team was laughing, I'd pretend he was laughing at me or the Bears," Butkus said. "It always worked for me."

Butkus only knew one speed—all out. When knee problems slowed him down, he retired at age 31.

27

The number of fumbles that Butkus recovered in his career, including seven as a rookie. Few defensive players ever recover so many fumbles.

Chicago Bears linebacker Dick Butkus (51) gets ready to make a tackle against the Los Angeles Rams.

DICK BUTKUS

Position: Linebacker

Hometown: Chicago, Illinois

College: University of Illinois

Height, Weight: 6-foot-3, 245 pounds

Birth Date: December 9, 1942

Team: Chicago Bears (1965–73)

All-Pro: 1965, 1968, 1969, 1970, 1972

Pro Bowls: 1965, 1966, 1967, 1968, 1969, 1970, 1971, 1972

"MEAN" JOE
GREENE

Joe Greene really wasn't mean, as his nickname implies. He showed his fun side in a famous Coca-Cola commercial when he drank a boy's entire soda, and then gave the boy his jersey. On the field, though, Greene was tough. He was strong. He was smart. And he was unstoppable—from the first day he joined the Pittsburgh Steelers.

Greene was the top defensive rookie in the NFL in 1969. By 1972, he was named the league's best overall defensive player. He again earned that honor two years later.

"He's the best football player I've seen," Steelers coach Chuck Noll said. "There will never be another Joe Greene."

Hall of Fame defensive tackle "Mean" Joe Greene was at the center of Pittsburgh's "Steel Curtain" defense of the 1970s.

The Steelers built their "Steel Curtain" defense around Greene.

He not only stopped the run, he also was a strong pass rusher. He knocked down passes. And he even designed a new way of going against blockers. He would line up at an angle instead of straight on. It confused the guards and centers trying to stop him. Before they could figure it out, he was past them. He once used that tactic against the Houston Oilers to make five sacks in one game.

But Greene was most dominant in the postseason. In addition to all of his tackles, Greene had an interception and a fumble recovery in Super Bowl IX against the Minnesota Vikings. Many believe he should have been named the Most Valuable Player (MVP) of Pittsburgh's first championship.

4

The number of Super Bowls, in four tries, that Greene won. Before he joined the team, the Steelers had never won the NFL championship.

"Mean" Joe Greene (75) chases after a fumble during a 1979 game against the San Diego Chargers.

"MEAN" JOE GREENE

Position: Defensive Tackle

Hometown: Temple, Texas

College: University of North Texas

Height, Weight: 6-foot-4, 275 pounds

Birth Date: September 24, 1946

Team: Pittsburgh Steelers (1969–81)

All-Pro: 1969, 1972, 1973, 1974, 1977

Pro Bowls: 1969, 1970, 1971, 1972, 1973, 1974, 1975, 1976, 1978, 1979

Super Bowls: IX, X, XIII, XIV

LAWRENCE TAYLOR

No one was quite like Lawrence Taylor.
The man nicknamed "L. T." was one of the NFL's most dominant players from the start of his career with the New York Giants. Taylor was the NFL's Defensive Rookie of the Year and Defensive Player of the Year in 1981. He then went on to be named the league's top defender in 1982 and 1986.

Taylor was so good that he won the NFL's MVP Award in 1986. That was only the second time a defensive player had earned the honor. Taylor had 20.5 sacks that season. His New York Giants also won the Super Bowl that year. It was the Giants' first championship in 30 years.

The New York Giants' Lawrence Taylor was one of the most dominant players of the 1980s.

Taylor was perhaps most famous for the strip-sack. He would streak around the outside of the offensive line from his right linebacker position. When he reached the quarterback, Taylor would sweep his arm down like a hammer hitting a nail. He'd hit the quarterback's arm or the ball and knock it loose. Taylor had 132.5 sacks in his career. That was the second most in football when he retired. Many of them came on that speedy move.

Taylor was so good that other teams began drafting players that could do the same things. Many of them were good, but L. T. was one of a kind.

"I always felt that I was better than the guy opposite me," Taylor said. "That's the only way to play the game, thinking you are the best out there."

10

The number of Pro Bowls in a row that Taylor made, from his rookie season through his second championship year with the Giants in 1990.

Lawrence Taylor, *left*, and Pepper Johnson, *right*, take down a Washington Redskins running back in 1990.

LAWRENCE TAYLOR

Position: Linebacker

Hometown: Williamsburg, Virginia

College: University of North Carolina

Height, Weight: 6-foot-3, 237 pounds

Birth Date: February 4, 1959

Team: New York Giants (1981–93)

All-Pro: 1981, 1982, 1983, 1984, 1985, 1986, 1988, 1989

Pro Bowls: 1981, 1982, 1983, 1984, 1985, 1986, 1987, 1988, 1989, 1990

Super Bowls: XXI, XXV

RONNIE LOTT

It's hard enough to make the All-Pro team at one position. Ronnie Lott did it at three.

Lott began his Hall of Fame career as a left cornerback for the San Francisco 49ers. As a rookie, he returned three interceptions for touchdowns. San Francisco won the first of its four Super Bowls with Lott in the lineup that season. That lineup included almost all young players.

"We were young," Lott said, "and maybe too young to know any better. So we expected to win right away."

They kept on winning, even as Lott switched to safety. He played free safety, where pass coverage is most important. He also was a strong safety later in his career, where run stopping is just as key. At each position, he made the Pro Bowl.

Ronnie Lott was a force in the San Francisco 49ers' secondary.

Lott was one of the hardest-hitting defensive backs ever. His best season was 1986. Lott led the NFL with 10 interceptions that year, returning one for a touchdown. He also forced three fumbles and made 77 tackles in 14 games.

Lott was a natural leader. Many of his teammates say he was their best teacher. Yet Lott never went into coaching.

Lott finished his career with 63 interceptions and five touchdowns. He also recovered 17 fumbles, forced 16 others, and was in on more than 1,100 tackles.

"He was the greatest defensive back ever," legendary 49ers coach Bill Walsh said, "and one of the greatest defensive players ever. Heck, one of the greatest players ever. . . . He just took over. He would challenge anyone."

79

The number of turnovers Lott forced during his career, with 16 forced fumbles and 63 interceptions. He scored five touchdowns on takeaways.

Ronnie Lott of the San Francisco 49ers takes down a Washington Redskins tight end during a 1990 game.

RONNIE LOTT

Positions: Cornerback, Safety

Hometown: Albuquerque, New Mexico

College: University of Southern California

Height, Weight: 6-feet, 203 pounds

Birth Date: May 8, 1959

Teams: San Francisco 49ers (1981–90)
Oakland Raiders (1991–92)
New York Jets (1993–94)

All-Pro: 1981, 1986, 1987, 1989, 1990, 1991

Pro Bowls: 1981, 1982, 1983, 1984, 1986, 1987, 1988, 1989, 1990, 1991

Super Bowls: XVI, XIX, XXIII, XXIV

REGGIE WHITE

It was the Philadelphia Eagles' 1987 season opener. Eagles defensive end Reggie White rushed into the Washington Redskins' backfield. The giant defender crashed into quarterback Doug Williams, knocking the ball loose. White reached down, grabbed it, and ran 70 yards for his first NFL touchdown. He then simply handed the ball back to the official.

White did not do sack dances. He did not stand over fallen quarterbacks, even though he knocked them down 198 times. White simply played football. And he did it so well that he was voted to 13 straight Pro Bowls.

Reggie White made a name for himself as a dominating defensive end for the Philadelphia Eagles in the 1980s.

White actually began his pro career in a rival league. When that league folded, he moved to Philadelphia to join the NFL. With the Eagles, White began a nine-year string with at least 11 sacks each year. A players' strike shortened the 1987 season. Nevertheless, White still had 21 sacks in 12 games. That earned him Defensive Player of the Year honors.

White, a deeply religious man, was nicknamed "The Minister of Defense." At age 17, he became an actual minister. And in 1993, White made another big move. Free agency had come to the NFL. White left the Eagles and signed with the Green Bay Packers.

It was not an easy choice, but it soon paid off. White helped the Packers win Super Bowl XXXI. He got three sacks against the New England Patriots in that game. That turned White into the minister of a *championship* defense.

198

The number of sacks White had in his 15 NFL seasons— the most for anyone at the time he retired after the 2000 season.

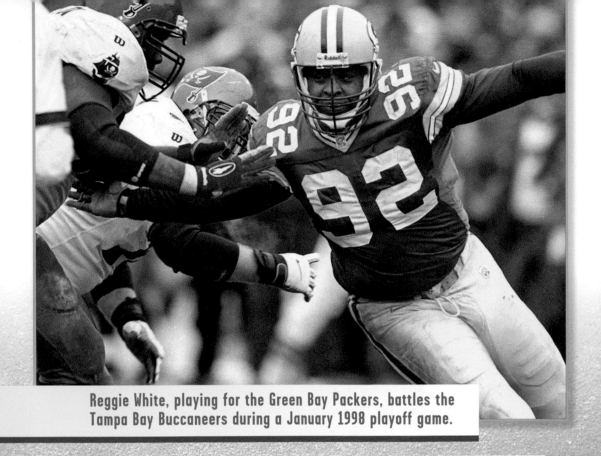

Reggie White, playing for the Green Bay Packers, battles the Tampa Bay Buccaneers during a January 1998 playoff game.

REGGIE WHITE

Position: Defensive End

Hometown: Chattanooga, Tennessee

College: University of Tennessee

Height, Weight: 6-foot-5, 291 pounds

Birth Date: December 19, 1961

Teams: Philadelphia Eagles (1985–92)
Green Bay Packers (1993–98)
Carolina Panthers (2000)

All-Pro: 1986, 1987, 1988, 1989, 1990, 1991, 1995, 1998

Pro Bowls: 1986, 1987, 1988, 1989, 1990, 1991, 1992, 1993, 1994, 1995, 1996, 1997, 1998

Super Bowls: XXXI, XXXII

BRUCE SMITH

Expectations were high for defensive end Bruce Smith after the Buffalo Bills picked him first overall in the 1985 NFL Draft. Yet after three games, Smith still had no sacks. Meanwhile, his Bills were 0–3.

That all changed in Smith's fourth game. He broke free for two sacks against the Minnesota Vikings. Those sacks would be the first in a record-setting career for Smith. Big, strong, and quick, Smith soon became one of the NFL's top pass rushers. He also learned how to stop the run, making him an all-around defender.

With Smith as the main man, Buffalo's defense helped the team reach four straight Super Bowls. No other team has ever done that through 2012.

Buffalo Bills defensive end Bruce Smith pushes away a Los Angeles Raiders blocker during a 1993 game.

"He's the best, and he'll tell you he's the best and mean it," said former teammate Darryl Talley. Smith never won the Super Bowl, though.

"I have so many great memories of being a Buffalo Bill," Smith said. "Those [Super Bowl losses] might not be part of those memories."

Smith had at least 10 sacks in 13 of his 19 seasons. His best move combined his power and speed. He would break quickly when the ball was snapped, shoving a blocker. At the same time, he would either run around the opponent or spin past him. Sometimes, he was so much stronger that he would simply knock over the blocker. Then, before anyone realized, Smith would be standing over the quarterback after another sack. It was just another day in the life of one of the NFL's best pass rushers.

200

The number of sacks Smith had in his career—the most of any player in NFL history through 2012. Surprisingly, Smith never led the league in sacks in a season.

Buffalo Bills defensive end Bruce Smith, *left*, and Phil Hansen combine for a sack in 1996.

BRUCE SMITH

Position: Defensive End

Hometown: Norfolk, Virginia

College: Virginia Tech

Height, Weight: 6-foot-4, 262 pounds

Birth Date: June 18, 1963

Teams: Buffalo Bills (1985–99)
Washington Redskins (2000–03)

All-Pro: 1987, 1988, 1990, 1993, 1994, 1995, 1996, 1997

Pro Bowls: 1987, 1988, 1989, 1990, 1992, 1993, 1994, 1995, 1996, 1997, 1998

Super Bowls: XXV, XXVI, XXVII, XXVIII

ROD WOODSON

Had Rod Woodson skipped pro football, he might have run in the Olympic Games. In fact, before he joined the Pittsburgh Steelers as a first-round draft pick in 1987, Woodson was running in track meets in Europe as a hurdler.

In college at Purdue, Woodson played offense and defense. But the Steelers saw him as a cornerback. He played a combination of that position and safety during his 17 seasons in the NFL. He also was a great kick returner. In 1993, he was voted the league's top defensive player.

Woodson played in three Super Bowls for three teams. His only victory came with the Baltimore Ravens after the 2000 season. He also played in the Super Bowl with the Oakland Raiders after the 2002 season.

Pittsburgh Steelers defensive back Rod Woodson waits to make a play against the Los Angeles Rams in 1993.

Woodson's most remarkable Super Bowl appearance came after the 1995 season. Woodson tore the ACL in his knee during the season opener that year. Doctors said he needed a year to recover. But Woodson worked hard to return that same season. Steelers coach Bill Cowher kept a roster spot open for Woodson, believing his star player would make it back. And he did. Woodson was able to play in the Super Bowl just four-and-a-half months after his injury.

"I can't imagine a coach today doing that," Woodson said in 2009.

Twice, Woodson led the league in interceptions. When he retired, he held the record for yards on interception returns.

103

The total number of interceptions (71) and fumble recoveries (32) by Woodson. He scored 13 touchdowns on turnovers, 12 on interceptions and one on a fumble.

Woodson was so good that he was chosen for the NFL's all-time team even while he was still playing.

Rod Woodson celebrates with Oakland Raiders fans after returning an interception for a touchdown in 2002.

ROD WOODSON

Positions: Cornerback, Safety, Returner

Hometown: Fort Wayne, Indiana

College: Purdue University

Height, Weight: 5-foot-11, 205 pounds

Birth Date: March 10, 1965

Teams: Pittsburgh Steelers (1987–96)
San Francisco 49ers (1997)
Baltimore Ravens (1998–2001)
Oakland Raiders (2002–03)

All-Pro: 1989, 1990, 1992, 1993, 1994, 2002

Pro Bowls: 1989, 1990, 1991, 1992, 1993, 1994, 1996, 1999, 2000, 2001, 2002

Super Bowls: XXX, XXXV, XXXVII

DEION SANDERS

They called him "Neon Deion" and "Prime Time." "Mr. Do-Everything" would have worked, too.

Deion Sanders was one of the NFL's best cover cornerbacks. He had such good hands that he not only picked off 53 passes, but he also played receiver. Sanders caught 60 balls and had three touchdowns on offense to go with his nine touchdowns on defense. He returned punts and kickoffs, too, scoring nine times on those. Sanders even played Major League Baseball.

When he entered the Pro Football Hall of Fame in 2011, Sanders said he wanted to be on the field, no matter what he was doing.

"Just playing, man," Sanders said with a big smile. "Nothing beats just playing."

Deion Sanders loved the spotlight. He got plenty of it with his strong play over the years in the NFL.

While Sanders never was much of a tackler, he rarely needed to be one.
Players he covered caught very few passes. And if the speedy, slippery Sanders got his hands on the ball—watch out!

After the 1994 season, Sanders won his first Super Bowl with the San Francisco 49ers. He then helped the Dallas Cowboys win the Super Bowl the next year. Even though he played for five NFL teams, Sanders always had a soft spot for Atlanta. When he accepted his Hall of Fame ring at an Atlanta Falcons home game, he asked fans, "What time is it?" The fans yelled, "Prime Time!"

To which Sanders said: "I love you. This is my home. I'm a Falcon."

.533

Sanders's batting average in the World Series for the Atlanta Braves in 1992. Along with his Hall of Fame football career, Sanders played Major League Baseball for nine years.

Deion Sanders, playing with the Dallas Cowboys, intercepts a pass against the Oakland Raiders in 1995.

DEION SANDERS

Positions: Cornerback, Wide Receiver, Returner

Hometown: Fort Myers, Florida

College: Florida State University

Height, Weight: 6-foot-1, 195 pounds

Birth Date: August 9, 1967

Teams: Atlanta Falcons (1989–93)
San Francisco 49ers (1994)
Dallas Cowboys (1995–99)
Washington Redskins (2000)
Baltimore Ravens (2004–05)

All-Pro: 1992, 1993, 1994, 1996, 1997, 1998

Pro Bowls: 1991, 1992, 1993, 1994, 1996, 1997, 1998, 1999

Super Bowls: XXIX, XXX

RAY LEWIS

Here comes Ray Lewis out of the tunnel. His Baltimore Ravens are about to kick off Super Bowl XXXV against the New York Giants. He's almost ready to play.

But first, he dances.

Lewis struts. He pounds his chest. He swivels his hips. He pounds the ground. The fans rock the stadium with their cheers. Now he's ready!

Never was Lewis better than in that 2000 season. On the field he always used his strength, quickness, smarts, courage—and a dose of nastiness. In 2000, the middle linebacker anchored one of the NFL's best-ever defenses. He also was the MVP in that Super Bowl XXXV win over the Giants.

Ray Lewis was the Baltimore Ravens' emotional leader for 17 seasons.

Lewis played with a scowl on his face and a wild look in his eyes.

He made tackles in the backfield or covered receivers on pass plays. He forced fumbles. And he encouraged teammates to always give that little extra.

156

The number of tackles Lewis had in 1997—a career high. It was just his second year with the Ravens and the first season in which he played the full schedule of 16 games.

"I've always played with heart and passion," Lewis said. "It's the only way I know how."

Lewis starred in the NFL for 17 seasons, all with the Ravens. He made the Pro Bowl in all 13 seasons in which he was healthy enough to play a full schedule. Lewis was the NFL's Defensive Player of the Year in 2000 and 2003.

Even when he was hurt and unable to play, Lewis stood on the sideline pumping his fists, waving his arms, and supporting his teammates. And he went out of the league on top. Lewis retired after leading the Ravens to victory in Super Bowl XLVII.

Ray Lewis tackles an Indianapolis Colts tight end during a January 2013 playoff game.

RAY LEWIS

Position: Linebacker

Hometown: Bartow, Florida

College: University of Miami (Florida)

Height, Weight: 6-foot-1, 245 pounds

Birth Date: May 15, 1975

Team: Baltimore Ravens (1996–2012)

All-Pro: 1999, 2000, 2001, 2003, 2004, 2008, 2009

Pro Bowls: 1997, 1998, 1999, 2000, 2001, 2003, 2004, 2006, 2007, 2008, 2009, 2010, 2011

Super Bowls: XXXV, XLVII

ED REED

The Philadelphia Eagles had the ball at the Baltimore Ravens' 1-foot line. The Eagles decided to pass. Big mistake.

Ravens safety Ed Reed saw it coming. He cut in front of the receiver deep in the Baltimore end zone and picked off the pass. Then he took off. Down the right sideline Reed sped. Three Eagles missed the tackle. And 107 yards later, a tired Reed was in the other end zone with the longest interception runback in NFL history.

"Ed Reed is just one of the greatest ballplayers I've ever seen," Ravens linebacker Ray Lewis said after the play in 2008. Reed also had the second-longest interception return, 106 yards in 2004. That year, he was named the league's top defensive player.

Ed Reed celebrates after returning an interception 107 yards for a touchdown in 2008 against the Philadelphia Eagles.

What's odd about Reed is that he isn't the fastest safety. He's not the hardest hitter or the strongest player, either. But he might be the smartest safety—ever.

Reed can read what offenses want to do from the way the players line up. He then goes where the play is headed and stops it. He has led the NFL in interceptions three times. However, he also has been fined many times for nasty hits.

Reed had long been a key player on the Ravens' traditionally strong defense. After the 2012 season he finally won his first title. Reed had a key interception when the Ravens beat the San Francisco 49ers in Super Bowl XLVII.

"He just does things that nobody else at that position does or I don't know if they've ever done it," New England Patriots coach Bill Belichick said. "He's special. He's really special."

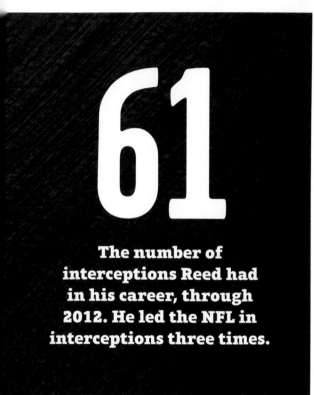

61

The number of interceptions Reed had in his career, through 2012. He led the NFL in interceptions three times.

Baltimore Ravens safety Ed Reed tackles a Denver Broncos wide receiver during a January 2013 playoff game.

ED REED

Position: Safety

Hometown: St. Rose, Louisiana

College: University of Miami (Florida)

Height, Weight: 5-foot-11, 200 pounds

Birth Date: September 11, 1978

Team: Baltimore Ravens (2002–)

All-Pro: 2004, 2006, 2007, 2008, 2010

Pro Bowls: 2003, 2004, 2006, 2007, 2008, 2009, 2010, 2011, 2012

Super Bowl: XLVII

PATRICK WILLIS

Patrick Willis often is compared to Ray Lewis. That makes Willis smile. "Very cool. Ray Lewis has been the best for so long," Willis said in 2011. The two great linebackers met for the final time in Super Bowl XLVII. Lewis retired after his Baltimore Ravens beat Willis's San Francisco 49ers.

Lewis's retirement means Willis probably is the best linebacker in pro football these days. He's been the main man in the 49ers shutdown 3–4 defense since his first pro season.

Willis was a first-round draft pick in 2007 out of Mississippi. He brought his speed, smarts, and hard work to the 49ers and was a starter from Day 1. Willis made 137 tackles in 2007 and was named Defensive Rookie of the Year. He had more than 100 tackles in each of the next three seasons, too.

Linebacker Patrick Willis has been a force for the San Francisco 49ers' defense since 2007.

In Willis's second season with the 49ers, Hall of Fame linebacker Mike Singletary became head coach. Willis reminded many of Singletary because of his focus and his ability to constantly be around the ball.

One of Willis's greatest skills is stripping the ball. He forced 14 fumbles in his first six seasons. He used his hands, arms, shoulders, helmet—whatever it took—to knock the ball free. He also recovered five fumbles.

"He's a big part of this team. He's our leader," 49ers tailback Frank Gore said. "I feel real good with 52 [Willis's jersey number] on the field."

Who on the 49ers wouldn't?

137

The number of tackles Willis made as a rookie in 2007 to earn All-Pro honors. He also assisted on 37 tackles that year.

Patrick Willis sacks Green Bay Packers quarterback Aaron Rodgers during a 49ers playoff win in January 2013.

PATRICK WILLIS

Position: Linebacker

Hometown: Bruceton, Tennessee

College: University of Mississippi

Height, Weight: 6-foot-1, 242 pounds

Birth Date: January 25, 1985

Team: San Francisco 49ers (2007–)

All-Pro: 2007, 2009, 2010, 2011, 2012

Pro Bowls: 2007, 2008, 2009, 2010, 2011, 2012

Super Bowl: XLVII

CLAY MATTHEWS

Talk about football family trees. Clay Matthews III might come from the greatest football family tree of all. At the top of the tree is grandfather Clay Matthews Sr. He spent four seasons in the NFL. Clay's dad, Clay Matthews Jr., played 19 seasons in the league. And his uncle, Bruce Matthews, was a Hall of Fame offensive lineman for 19 seasons. Plus Clay's brother Casey Matthews and cousin Kevin Matthews have also played in the NFL.

Clay Matthews III was one of the three standout linebackers at the University of Southern California who were drafted in the first round in 2009. But he was the first of those three to make it to a Super Bowl, which he won in February 2011 with the Green Bay Packers.

Green Bay Packers linebacker Clay Matthews III comes from a football family.

Matthews sometimes is used in pass coverage because of his speed and size. But he has done his best work as a pass rusher. He had 42.5 sacks in his first four seasons. His career-high was 13.5 in 2010.

With his blond hair flowing out of his helmet, Matthews is easy to spot on the field and on TV—he does many commercials.

"I don't know that we all anticipated the kind of success and kind of rock star quality he has right now," uncle Bruce Matthews said, "but it's really fun to watch, and I'm very proud of him."

There is another good way to spot Matthews: look for the ball. Matthews will be somewhere near it.

42.5

The number of sacks Matthews had in his first four seasons, an average of more than 10 a year, even though he missed six games in those years.

Green Bay Packers fans have gotten used to Clay Matthews's trademark sack celebration.

CLAY MATTHEWS

Position: Linebacker

Hometown: Los Angeles, California

College: University of Southern California

Height, Weight: 6-foot-3, 246 pounds

Birth date: May 14, 1986

Team: Green Bay Packers (2009–)

All-Pro: 2010

Pro Bowls: 2009, 2010, 2011, 2012

Super Bowl: XLV

HONORABLE MENTIONS

Chuck Bednarik – He played center and linebacker and led the Philadelphia Eagles to the NFL title in 1960.

Buck Buchanan – An unblockable defensive tackle, he did not miss a game in all 13 years he played for the Kansas City Chiefs beginning in 1963.

Jack Ham – A do-everything linebacker for four Pittsburgh Steelers championship teams of the 1970s, he had 32 interceptions and 21 fumble recoveries.

Ken Houston – He was the best safety in the American Football League and then in the NFL after the leagues merged in 1970. He had 49 interceptions and nine touchdowns.

Jack Lambert – The toughest of the tough guys on Pittsburgh's "Steel Curtain" in the 1970s, he was a linebacker who never stopped hitting hard.

Bob Lilly – The first great Dallas Cowboy, Lilly remains as popular as ever nearly 40 years after retiring.

Ray Nitschke – As the leader of the Green Bay Packers' great defenses in the 1960s at middle linebacker, he won five NFL titles.

Merlin Olsen – He made 14 straight Pro Bowls at defensive tackle and was the anchor of "Fearsome Foursome" for the Los Angeles Rams of the 1960s.

Alan Page – The defensive tackle on the Minnesota Vikings "Purple People Eaters" defensive line of the 1970s became the first defensive player to be named NFL MVP in 1971.

Mel Renfro – The great cornerback had 52 interceptions and was a dangerous kick returner for Dallas' "Doomsday Defense" of the 1960s and 1970s.

Brian Urlacher – The man in the middle of the Chicago Bears' defense in the early 2000s.

GLOSSARY

draft
A system used by professional sports leagues to select new players in order to spread incoming talent among all teams. The NFL Draft is held each April.

free agency
A system in which players who are not signed to a contract are allowed to sign a new contract with any team in the league.

merged
United into a single body.

playoffs
A series of single-elimination games amongst the best teams after the regular season that determines which two teams meet in the Super Bowl.

Pro Bowl
An annual All-Star game that takes place one week before the Super Bowl.

retired
When one has officially ended his career.

rookie
A player's first year in the NFL.

strike
A work stoppage by employees in protest of working conditions.

FOR MORE INFORMATION

Further Reading

Dunn, Jeremy. *Superstars of Pro Football: Ray Lewis*. Broomall, PA: Mason Crest Publishers, 2007.

Gramling, Gary. *Sports Illustrated Kids 1st and 10: Top 10 Lists of Everything in Football*. New York: Sports Illustrated, 2011.

Polzer, Tim. *NFL Reader: Defense*. New York: Scholastic Inc., 2011.

Web Links

To learn more about the NFL's best defensive players, visit ABDO Publishing Company online at **www.abdopublishing.com**. Web sites about the NFL's best defensive players are featured on our Book Links page. These links are routinely monitored and updated to provide the most current information available.

INDEX

Atlanta Falcons, 44, 45

Baltimore Ravens, 38, 41, 45, 46–48, 49, 50–52, 53, 54
Belichick, Bill, 52
Buffalo Bills, 34–36, 37
Butkus, Dick, 14–17

Carolina Panthers, 33
Chicago Bears, 14–16, 17
Chicago Cardinals, 9
Cowher, Bill, 40

Dallas Cowboys, 44, 45
Detroit Lions, 9

Gore, Frank, 56
Green Bay Packers, 32, 33, 58–60, 61
Greene, "Mean" Joe, 18–21

Halas, George, 16
Hall of Fame, 8, 10, 26, 42, 44, 56, 58
Houston Oilers, 20

Jones, David "Deacon," 10–13

Lane, Dick "Night Train," 6–9
Lewis, Ray, 46–49, 50, 54
Los Angeles Rams, 8, 9, 10–12, 13
Lott, Ronnie, 26–29

Major League Baseball, 42, 44
Matthews, Bruce, 58, 60
Matthews, Clay, III, 58–61
Matthews, Clay, Jr., 58
Matthews, Clay, Sr., 58
McDonald, Tommy, 8
Minnesota Vikings, 20, 34

New England Patriots, 32, 52
New York Giants, 22–24, 25, 46
New York Jets, 29
NFL Draft, 12, 16, 34, 38, 54, 58
NFL MVP Award, 22
Noll, Chuck, 18

Oakland Raiders, 29, 38, 41
Olsen, Merlin, 10

Philadelphia Eagles, 30–32, 33, 50
Pittsburgh Steelers, 18–20, 21, 38–40, 41

Reed, Ed, 50–53

San Diego Chargers, 12, 13
San Francisco 49ers, 26, 28, 29, 41, 44, 45, 52, 54–56, 57
Sanders, Deion, 42–45
Singletary, Mike, 56
Smith, Bruce, 34–37

Talley, Darryl, 36
Taylor, Lawrence, 22–25

Walsh, Bill, 28
Washington Redskins, 13, 30, 37, 45
White, Reggie, 30–33
Williams, Doug, 30
Willis, Patrick, 54–57
Woodson, Rod, 38–41

ABOUT THE AUTHOR

Barry Wilner has been a sportswriter for the Associated Press since 1976. He has written about every sport and has covered every Super Bowl since 1985. He has also covered the World Cup, the Stanley Cup Finals, the Summer and Winter Olympics, the Pan American Games, championship boxing matches, major golf and tennis tournaments, and auto races.